Signs in My World

Signs at the Park

By Mary Hill

Children's Press®
A Division of Scholastic Inc.
New York / Toronto / London / Auckland / Sydney
Mexico City / New Delhi / Hong Kong
Danbury, Connecticut

Photo Credits: Cover and all photos by Maura B. McConnell
Contributing Editor: Jennifer Silate
Book Design: Erica Clendening and Michelle Innes

Library of Congress Cataloging-in-Publication Data

Hill, Mary, 1977-
  Signs at the park / by Mary Hill.
  p. cm. — (Signs in my world)
  Summary: Sally explains the signs that she and her mother see while
walking their dog in a park, such as those that direct them to a trail
and show who can use that trail.
  ISBN 0-516-24273-3 (lib. bdg.) — ISBN 0-516-24365-9 (pbk.)
  1. Dog walking—Juvenile literature. 2. Parks—Juvenile literature.
  3. Signs and signboards—Juvenile literature. [1. Dog walking. 2.
Parks. 3. Signs and signboards.] I. Title. II. Series.

SF427.46 .H56 2003
302.23—dc21

                                                        2002009644

Contents

Hi, my name is Sally.

Mom and I are going to walk our dog in the **park**.

Our dog's name is Katie.

There are many **signs** in the park.

This sign says, "All Pets Must Be **Leashed**."

ALL PETS MUST BE LEASHED

I put a leash on Katie.

Now, we will go for a walk.

ALL PETS
MUST BE
LEASHED

9

We will walk on a **trail**.

There is a sign that says, "Trails."

TRAILS ↑

11

This sign tells us that there are trails ahead.

TRAILS ↑

13

There is a sign on the trail.

It has pictures of a car, a person, and a bike.

The picture of the car has a line through it.

15

This sign means that people can walk and ride bikes on the trail.

The sign also means that cars cannot go on the trail.

Multi-Use Trail

17

We are ready to go home.

Mom drives by a sign
that says, "**Exit.**"

The Exit sign shows us the way out of the park.

We saw many signs in the park today.

21

New Words

exit (**eg**-zit) the way out of a place

leashed (**leeshd**) having a strap, cord, or chain around an animal to control it

park (**park**) an area of land with trees, benches, and sometimes playgrounds, used by the public for recreation

signs (**sinez**) public notices that give information

trail (**trayl**) a track or path for people to follow

To Find Out More

Books

Letters from the Canyon
by Kathleen McAnally
Grand Canyon Association

Yellowstone National Park
by Cari Meister
Checkerboard Library

Web Site
Santa Clara Parks: Go Outside and Play
http://www.co.santa-clara.ca.us/parks/kids/kids.html
Learn about the different animals that are found in parks on this Web site.

Index

exit, 18, 20

leash, 8

park, 4, 6, 20
picture, 14

sign, 6, 10, 12,
14, 16, 18,
20

trail, 10, 12,
14, 16

About the Author
Mary Hill writes and edits children's books.

Reading Consultants

Kris Flynn, Coordinator, Small School District Literacy, The San Diego County Office of Education

Shelly Forys, Certified Reading Recovery Specialist, W.J. Zahnow Elementary School, Waterloo, IL

Sue McAdams, Former President of the North Texas Reading Council of the IRA, and Early Literacy Consultant, Dallas, TX